DATE DUE

Quentin Blake

COCKATOOS

Little, Brown and Company
Boston   Toronto   London

Other books by Quentin Blake:
Patrick
Jack and Nancy
Angelo
Snuff
Mister Magnolia
Quentin Blake's Nursery Rhyme Book
The Story of the Dancing Frog
Mrs Armitage on Wheels
Quentin Blake's ABC
All Join In

to my friends in France

29 122
E
BLA

First U.S. Edition
First published in Great Britain by Jonathan Cape Ltd.

Library of Congress
Cataloguing-in-Publication
information is available.

10 9 8 7 6 5 4 3 2 1

Printed in Hong Kong

Professor Dupont had ten cockatoos.
He was very proud of them.

Every morning he jumped out of bed.

He took a shower and
he brushed his teeth,

as he always did.

He got dressed and he tied his tie,
as he always did.

He adjusted his glasses,
as he always did.

And he went downstairs.

He went into the conservatory.
There were all his cockatoos,
        every single one.

Professor Dupont threw wide his arms.
He said: "Good morning,
        my fine feathered friends!"

Every morning he said the same thing.
The day came when the cockatoos thought they would go crazy if they had to listen to the same words once again.

They decided to have some fun with Professor Dupont. One after another they escaped through a broken pane of glass they had discovered in a corner of the conservatory.

Next morning Professor Dupont came into the
conservatory and threw wide his arms.
There was not a cockatoo in sight.

Where could all the cockatoos have gone?

Professor Dupont went into the dining room.
They weren't there.

He went to look in the kitchen.
Hortense the cook was there,
boiling an egg for his breakfast,
but there weren't any cockatoos.

He went to look in the bedroom.
They weren't there.

He looked in the bathroom.
They weren't there.

He looked in the toilet.
They weren't there.

He climbed a ladder
and shone his flashlight around the attic.
They weren't there.

He even climbed up to the roof.
But they weren't there.

Professor Dupont went to look in the garage.
His car was there,
but there weren't any cockatoos.

He went down to the cellar, but he couldn't see any cockatoos there, either.

Professor Dupont was at his wit's end.
He couldn't find his cockatoos anywhere.
Where could they possibly have gone?

Professor Dupont spent a restless night.

The next morning he jumped out of bed.
He took a shower and he brushed his teeth,
as he always did.

He got dressed and he tied his tie,
as he always did.

He adjusted his glasses,
as he always did.

And he went downstairs.

Professor Dupont went into the conservatory.
There were all his cockatoos, where they
always were – every single one!

Professor Dupont threw wide his arms.
He said: "Good morning,
my fine feathered friends!"

Some people never learn.